Contents

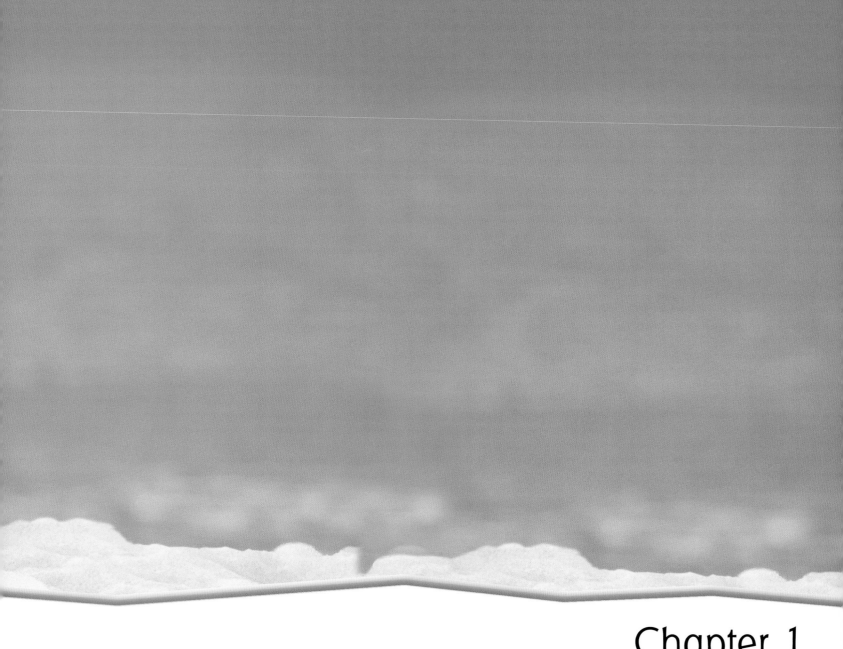

Chapter 1
A Penguin Story

Freezing Facts

The continent of Antarctica surrounds the South Pole and is the coldest, windiest place on Earth! It is almost completely covered with thick ice. Hundreds of thousands of penguins live there!

Birds That Don't Fly

Penguins are birds, but they cannot fly. They are too big and heavy, and their wings are too short for them to stay in the air.

It's the first day of winter on the continent of Antarctica. A group of emperor penguins huddle together for warmth. The penguins chatter and whistle excitedly. Any day now, the mother penguins will be ready to lay their eggs.

After Mama Penguin lays her egg, Papa Penguin rolls it carefully with his beak from her webbed feet to his own. Then he snuggles the precious bundle under a special feathered flap to keep it safe and warm. He says good-bye to Mama Penguin, who sets off on a very long walk to the sea to find food.

Papa Penguin shuffles gingerly inside the huddle, taking great care not to let his egg roll off his feet. At last it is time for Little Penguin to hatch!

Egg Shells

Penguin eggs can be white, tan, bluish, or greenish. The size varies according to the type of penguin. The eggs of emperor penguins are the size of grapefruits! It may take a chick three days to tap its way out of its egg.

When Mama Penguin comes back with food from the sea, she calls out to Papa Penguin by singing a song. It is the song she sang to Papa the first time they met. When Papa Penguin sings back, Mama Penguin is able to find him and Little Penguin in the crowded colony. Little Penguin is peeking out from his special place on his father's feet. The family is back together again!

Little Penguin grows very quickly. Soon he is too big to remain on his parents' feet. He joins a group of other penguin chicks, snuggling closely with them to stay safe and warm. Meanwhile, grown-up penguins keep a watchful eye on them.

Little Penguin's mother shows him how to use his beak to clean his feathers. Penguin chicks are covered with a special layer of fine, fluffy, soft feathers called "down."

Feet First

After baby penguins hatch from their eggs, they sit on their fathers' feet, where it is warm and cozy under the feathers of a special place called a "brood patch." The baby penguins have a great view from there, too!

After a few months, Little Penguin and the rest of the penguin chicks have grown enough waterproof feathers to be allowed into the water.

They follow their parents on a long walk to the sea, where they will learn to catch fish. It is fun to slide down the snowy hills on their stomachs!

As soon as the penguins reach the water, Little Penguin jumps in with all of his friends! At first, the penguin chicks are not very good swimmers. They watch how the grown-ups use their webbed feet and stiff wings like the oars of a boat to push through the water. Soon the chicks are diving and "flying" through the water, just like their parents.

The penguins spend many weeks at the sea, eating. When the air turns colder, they know winter is coming. By now, Little Penguin isn't a baby any longer! He looks just like his parents, except a bit shorter.

In a few years, Little Penguin will become a father himself—and balance an egg of his own on his feet!

Wild Words
A **rookery** *is the place where thousands of penguins gather to mate, lay their eggs, and raise their young.*

Chapter 2
Comical and Amazing

Cooling Off

Penguins are warm-blooded. Their body temperature is almost the same as yours! When they feel too hot, penguins extend their wings. This allows the extra heat to escape from both sides of their wings.

A penguin's webbed feet help steer in the water. Its sharp claws grip the icy ground.

Penguin Portrait

There are many different kinds of penguins living in different parts of the world, but they are all very much alike. They have black or dark blue backs and white undersides. Their short, wide legs and webbed feet are set back on their bodies so that the birds are able to stand up straight. Many people think penguins look like little men wearing tuxedos!

Penguins have other physical traits in common:

The **beak**, or **bill**, is short and sharp—good for catching fish.

The **wings** are short and the bones inside are flat to keep them from bending as the penguins push themselves through the water.

The puffy **chest** contains strong muscles that provide power to the wings.

The **tail** is used for balance on land and for steering in the water.

A pocket inside the penguin's throat, called a **crop**, stores food.

A flap of skin and feathers, called a **brood patch**, keeps the egg, and later the chick, warm and insulated.

Looking Good!

Like most birds, penguins clean their feathers regularly. This activity is called "preening." Preening is especially important for penguins after they have been in the water. Diving pushes the air out of their feathers, flattening them. Penguins then need to fluff their feathers up to help trap their body heat. As they preen, penguins rub oil onto their feathers with their beak to make them waterproof. The oil is made in a gland near the tail.

Feather Fluff

Penguins molt, or lose, their feathers once a year and replace them with new feathers. It takes three weeks for the new feathers to grow in. During this time, a penguin cannot go into the water, and so it does not eat. A penguin uses up a lot of energy while molting, often losing half its body weight.

Asleep on Their Feet

Some penguins sleep standing up. They may tuck their heads under one of their wings. Penguins can also sleep in the water!

Preening helps penguins keep their feathers windproof and waterproof.

Layered for Warmth

Penguins have two layers of feathers that help them stay warm in freezing-cold water. The outer layer of waterproof feathers keeps penguins' skin dry. The inner layer of feathers traps warm air against their bodies. Beneath the feathers is a layer of fat, called "blubber," which offers additional protection.

Water Safe

The colors of a penguin's body help protect it in the water. The white underside makes the penguin difficult for a predator to see from below. Its dark back makes the penguin difficult to see from above.

With their stiff wings and fast speed, penguins look as if they are flying through the water!

Birds That Swim

Penguins can't fly, but they are super swimmers. They are heavier than flying birds, which lets them dive below the ocean's surface. Penguins have a sleek, streamlined shape that glides easily through the water. Their tail and webbed feet help them steer. Stiff wings act like paddles, pushing the penguins forward.

Penguins move more quickly in water than they do on land. Their average swimming speed is about 8 miles per hour—3 miles per hour faster than a human swimmer!

Do penguins breathe underwater?

Penguins can't breathe underwater. They must come to the surface to breathe in air. Penguins swim for long distances and for long periods of time by "porpoising." They leap gracefully above the water to breathe and then dive back in, as do dolphins and porpoises.

Because penguins must come to the surface often, their dives are short and shallow. The emperor penguin is the exception. It is a champion diver that can go 870 feet deep. That's about the same as 87 floors of a building!

On the Move

Penguins spend most of their lives in the ocean. The rest of the time they are on land, traveling to and from or staying at their rookery—the place penguins mate and raise their young.

Since penguins don't fly, how do they get from the water onto land? Where the coastline is like a beach, penguins can simply walk onto land. But when the coast is rocky or high because of snow and ice, the penguins jump straight out of the water and land flat on their feet, like cats! Adélie penguins are only 2 feet tall, but they can leap three times that high to get from the water onto land. That's the equivalent of you jumping to the top of a swing set!

On snowy terrain, penguins "toboggan"—they slide on their bellies, using their wings and feet like ski poles to push themselves down hills and across the snow, often for miles and miles. During long journeys, penguins take turns being first. The leader flops onto its stomach and makes a track in the snow, which the others follow. This saves energy, because the other penguins don't need to create tracks for themselves.

Upstanding

Penguins are able to stand upright because their legs are set so far back on their bodies, unlike the legs of other birds.

Penguins frequently march in long, regular lines like soldiers. They walk with their webbed feet flat on the icy ground, swaying slightly from side to side. This waddling effect can look very comical.

Chapter 3
Group Living

How do penguins find each other in a huge group?

Different species of penguins use different sorts of sounds, including trumpeting, cooing, singing, and croaking. Parents and chicks also recognize each other by sight.

Huddling for Warmth

In the southern half of the world, where penguins live, the seasons are the opposite of what they are in the northern hemisphere, where we live. For the thousands of penguins living in Antarctica, the harsh and terrible winter begins in May and ends around September. Summer begins in October or November and ends in February or March.

Living in large groups gives penguins a good way to stay warm. Emperor penguins form huddles during the fierce and freezing winter weather. They take turns standing in the middle, where it is warmest, and on the outside, where it is coldest. The temperature inside a huddle can be more than 70 degrees Fahrenheit! On exceptionally cold days, penguins huddle very close together, reducing the amount of heat they lose by as much as 50 percent.

Living in a large group also makes it possible for penguins to live on the limited amount of land suitable for them. Penguin colonies are like cities where humans live, with hundreds of thousands of birds sharing space. Since penguins communicate with their voices, imagine how noisy penguin colonies can be!

Wild Words

*A **huddle** is a very big group of penguins.*

Safety in Numbers

Living in a huge group greatly increases an individual penguin's chances of survival against predators. While one penguin by itself does not pose a threat to an attacker, thousands of penguins together are a nice show of force.

Leopard seals, fur seals, sea lions, sharks, and killer whales all hunt penguins in the water. Another threat to penguins is water pollution by humans.

Penguin eggs and babies are vulnerable to attacks from birds that swoop down from the air, such as skuas, sheathbills, and giant petrels. These birds usually prey on chicks that have strayed from the group or that are weak or sickly.

Beak Defense!

When penguins see a bird flying in to attack, they raise an alarm call to the colony. At once, thousands of beaks turn upward to the sky. Faced with such a pointed defense, smart predators usually fly away.

Thousands of pairs of eyes are quite a bit better than one pair when it comes to spotting attackers.

Jumping In

When a group of penguins reaches the "shoreline"—actually, the edge of the ice—the birds don't always rush into the water right away, even if they are very hungry. Often, one brave bird jumps in first to make sure the water is safe and no predator is nearby that might attack. Then the rest of the penguins jump in, sometimes all at once!

Sea Food

Penguins eat only when they are at sea. They don't eat when they are on land. Penguins that live in zoos must be trained to eat on land.

Penguins eat krill—a tiny, shrimplike animal—crabs, shrimp, squids, and fish, but they will eat whatever they find in the ocean.

Penguins have a huge appetite. Swimming uses up a lot of their energy. Adélie penguins, for example, eat an average of one shrimp every six seconds!

Penguins don't have teeth. They swallow their food whole. Their tongues are spiny and their jaws are strong, allowing penguins to hang onto slippery fish.

Unlike humans, penguins can drink salty seawater without becoming sick. Special glands at the tips of their beaks remove the salt, which flows down grooves to the end of the beaks and drips off.

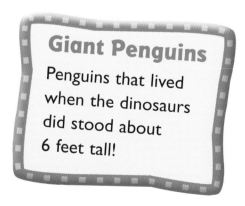

Giant Penguins

Penguins that lived when the dinosaurs did stood about 6 feet tall!

Chapter 4

Parents and Chicks

Egg Sitter

Penguin dads, like this rockhopper father, keep their eggs safe and warm until the baby penguin is hatched.

Mother and father penguins share the responsibility of raising their little ones.

Going Home

Every year, penguins return to the place where they were born—to molt their feathers, mate, lay their eggs, and raise their young. Some penguins must travel great distances to their home. Adélie penguins have walked more than 200 miles to reach their breeding ground! Scientists believe penguins use the position of the sun, stars, and perhaps some familiar places along the way to find their home.

Usually, the males arrive first to stake out their nesting site, which is sometimes a patch of ground the size of a bath mat! Most penguins build nests on the ground, using pebbles, sticks, grass, and seaweed. Others build nests underground. Emperor penguins do not make nests at all. The father penguin puts the egg on his feet and keeps it safe and warm in a special place under his feathers called a "brood patch."

One in a Million

How does a penguin find its mate among the thousands of identical-looking penguins in the rookery? By listening for its mate's song. Every penguin has its own song, which its mate can recognize.

When the pair meet, they stand facing each other, raise their beaks in the air, and weave their heads back and forth together.

Penguin Chicks

After hatching from the eggs, penguin chicks stay on their parents' feet for warmth and protection. By the time they are about seven weeks old, most chicks have grown too big to remain with their parents. They join a nursery group of twenty or more other young penguins, called a "crèche," where they huddle together for warmth. In some species, the crèche is guarded by several adult penguins on the lookout for predators.

Young penguins are completely dependent on their parents for food—even after they have grown too big to stand on their parents' feet. They cannot enter the water until their fluffy down feathers are replaced by grown-up ones. This can be as short as seven weeks or as long as thirteen months. Once the chick has fledged (grown in its adult feathers), it can go into the water to feed itself.

Feed Me!

A penguin chick's parents take turns going to the sea and bringing back food for their baby. The parent stores the food in its crop, a pocket inside the penguin's throat used especially for this purpose. The parent regurgitates the food directly into the chick's mouth.

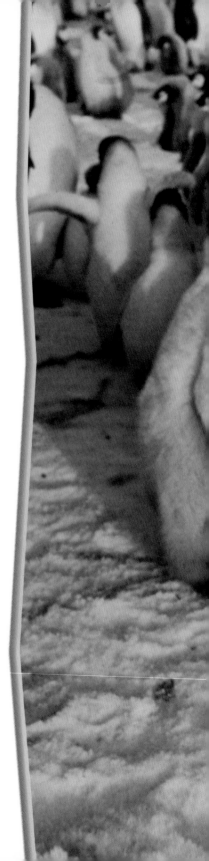

When young penguins are too big to stay on their parents' feet, they huddle together in a small group.

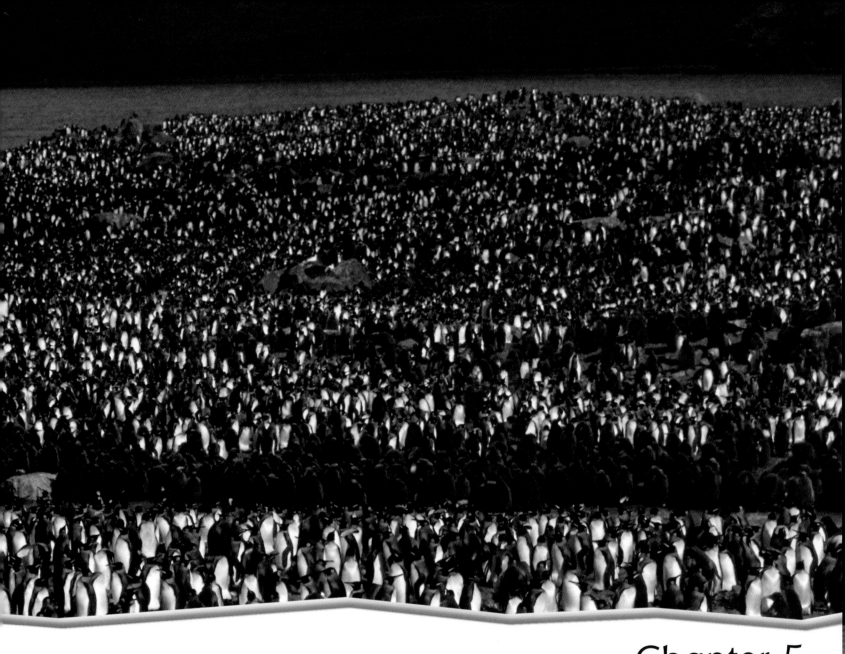

Chapter 5
Penguins in the World

Wild and Crazy Feathers

Rockhopper penguins are named for the way they get around— they hop from rock to rock! They have a crest of feathers on the top of their heads with a plume of yellow ones.

Rockhoppers live on the rocky islands of the sub-Antarctic and on warmer islands in the Indian and South Atlantic oceans.

Adélie penguins are named after Adélie Dumont d'Urville, the wife of the French explorer of Antarctica. They are the smallest of the penguins living in the Antarctic — 18 to 24 inches high and 8 to 10 pounds.

All Kinds of Penguins

There are 17 different kinds of penguins. The largest, the emperor penguin, is about the size of a fourth grader!

Emperor penguins are 36 to 44 inches high and weigh 60 to 90 pounds. They live only in Antarctica where temperatures can be -80 degrees Fahrenheit and the winds more than 100 miles per hour.

King penguins are the second largest and look a lot like emperor penguins. Kings have bright yellow feathers on their breast. They are about 37 inches high and weigh 30 to 35 pounds. King penguins live on the sub-Antarctic and Antarctic islands.

Little Blues are the smallest of all the penguins. They are only 10 to 12 inches high and weigh just 2 to 3 pounds. Little Blues can be found only in Australia and New Zealand. Of all the penguins, they sing the most.

Galápagos penguins live on the hot, tropical islands of the Galápagos, off the coast of Ecuador in South America, where the temperature can be more than 100 degrees Fahrenheit. Galápagos penguins are about 21 inches high and weigh 5 to 6 pounds.

Chinstrap penguins are named after the black line that runs under their chin. Chinstraps stand about 30 inches high and weigh about 10 pounds. They live only in the Antarctic and have pink feet.

Where Penguins Live

All penguins live in the Southern Hemisphere, below Earth's equator. Many live where it is icy and freezing cold. Others live where the temperature is mild or even tropical!

Penguins are sea birds. They spend most of their life in the water, which is where they eat. Once a year, they return to the place on land where they were born (usually on an island), to mate and raise their baby chicks.

Fast Facts About Emperor Penguins

Scientific name	*Aptenodytes forsteri*
Class	Aves
Order	Sphenisciformes
Weight	60 to 90 pounds
Height	3 to 4 feet
Eggs	1 each year
Swimming speed	8 miles per hour
Life span	up to 20 years
Habitat	ocean, coastline of ice-covered Antarctica

Royal penguins have a crest of yellow feathers on their heads. Royals mate only on Macquarie Island, which is between Australia and Antarctica.

Glossary of Wild Words

blubber   a layer of fat under the skin of sea animals that keeps them warm

breeding ground   a place where animals go to mate, give birth, and raise their young

chick   a young penguin

crèche   a group of young penguins huddling together for protection and warmth

down   soft and fluffy feathers

equator   an imaginary line around the earth that is halfway between the North Pole and the South Pole

flipper   a wide flat limb used for swimming

gland   a part of the body that makes chemicals an animal needs to live

hatch   to be born by breaking out of an egg

huddle   a very big group of penguins

incubation   the time spent warming an egg until it hatches

krill   a tiny shrimplike animal living in the sea that penguins eat

migrate   to go from one place to another at certain times of the year to find food or to mate and give birth

molt   to shed old feathers and grow new ones

porpoise   to leap above the water and breathe in air before diving into the water again

predator   an animal that hunts and eats other animals

prey   an animal that is hunted by another for food

regurgitate   to bring swallowed food back into the mouth

rookery   a place where thousands of penguins gather to mate, lay their eggs, and raise their young

species   a group of plants or animals that are the same in many ways

warm-blooded   having a body temperature that stays the same even when the outside temperature changes

Index